The Song of Sky and Sand

Written by **Stephen Davies**

Illustrated by **Beidi Guo**

ISBN-13: 978-0-328-83289-7
ISBN-10: 0-328-83289-8
10   19
Printed in Mexico

In the north of Mali, in shimmering West African heat, a donkey cart rattled along a sandy track. Perched on the front of the cart, leaning against a big empty water barrel, sat Ramata. She gazed down at the ground, watching how the legs of the donkey's shadow lengthened as the afternoon wore on.

On the sandy plain to her right stood a herd of bony cows. Their sad eyes seemed to ask, *Do you think it will rain today?*

Do you think it will rain today? Every day for the last two months, Ramata had asked or heard that question, and every day she had been disappointed. The sky remained cloudless. The ground remained dry. Last year's grass was gone, down to the very last straw, and without rain this year's grass would never sprout.

"Are we there yet?"

The sudden voice in Ramata's ear made her jump. "Yusuf!" she hissed. "I thought you were asleep. Yes, we're almost there. Look." She pointed toward a cluster of huts up ahead. The roofs were neatly thatched, and the mud-brick walls glowed orange in the early evening sun.

A little way in front of the huts stood a rusty pump.

Cousin Yusuf's eyes narrowed. "That's strange," he said. "There's no one at the pump today, except that little boy."

It was strange indeed. Every day for two months, Ramata and Yusuf had brought the donkey cart the two miles to Houndi and filled a barrel from the water pump. Whatever time of day they arrived, the pump was always crowded. Sometimes they had to wait hours for their turn to draw water.

"The pump's worn out!" shouted the boy when he saw them coming. "Overuse, they say. And it's going to take two weeks to fix!"

"Two weeks!" cried Ramata. "But this is our only supply of drinking water! What will my family back in Simbi say when I tell them we can't get water for two weeks?"

The boy shrugged. "Perhaps it will rain tomorrow."

"Perhaps," muttered Ramata. She turned her donkey around.

"I'm sorry, Donkey," she said. "I know you're thirsty. We are too. We'll find some water somewhere else, I promise."

They started the journey back to Simbi.

On the way out of Houndi, they passed an old woman pounding grain with a wooden stick. *Pok-pok, pok-pok* went her heavy pounding stick. As the cart rattled past, Ramata caught part of a line from the old woman's song: *"Lift your eyes from the dust-dry sand . . ."*

There was more to the mysterious song—something about summer and giants—but the words were drowned out by the wheels of Ramata's donkey cart.

CHAPTER 2

After dinner that night, Ramata's family sat around the fire in their yard.

"Our wells have all dried up," Ramata's father said, "and now the pump in Houndi is broken. If our cows and goats don't drink, they will die. Later tonight I will gather the animals and start walking south toward Burkina Faso. They say some rain has fallen there."

"What about the rest of us?" Ramata's mother asked. "What about the women and children, and the elderly? How are we to drink? We can't all walk to Burkina Faso—it's fifty miles from here!"

There was a long silence, and then Ramata's grandma stood up. "We will follow the old ways," she said. "We will dig at the base of acacia trees. We can suck water from the roots."

Grandma then waved goodnight and shuffled over to her sleeping mat. She climbed inside the mosquito net and lay down with a quiet groan beneath the shining stars.

Ramata went to lie down beside her grandma. It was cooler to sleep outside, but Ramata was still hot and thirsty.

"Grandma, I'm scared," she whispered.
"I don't want to suck water from tree roots.
The ground is so dry these days. Will there
even be any water left in the roots?"

"There, there, girl," Grandma whispered.
"We will look after each other. Everything
will be all right."

Ramata lay down and began to sing.
"Lift your eyes from the dust-dry sand . . ."

"What's that?" Grandma's voice interrupted Ramata. "What's that you're singing?"

"I don't really know," murmured Ramata. "It's just a song I heard someone singing today."

"I know that song," said Grandma, "but I haven't heard it since I was a little girl!" She began to sing softly in the darkness:

"Lift your eyes from the dust-dry sand to summer's breaking dawn.
Dry lips may drink from the crooked hand beneath the giant's sword."

"It's beautiful," said Ramata. "What does it mean?"

"Nothing," chuckled Grandma. "It's just a silly pounding song my grandmother taught me when I was small. We used to sing it as we prepared the dinner."

And with that they went to sleep.

CHAPTER 3

"Yusuf! Yusuf! Wake up!" Ramata called impatiently outside her cousin's door.

It was only five o'clock in the morning, but at long last, the door swung open. Yusuf shuffled out into the cool morning light, yawning.

"What's wrong?" he muttered.

"It's a riddle!" Ramata shouted.

"What's a riddle?" said Yusuf wearily.

"The pounding song that woman was singing yesterday, when we were on the way home from Houndi. Grandma told me the words last night, and then this morning I opened my eyes and looked east and suddenly it all made sense. It's a riddle from the old days. It's about where to find water in times of drought!"

Yusuf rubbed his eyes and scowled at her. "That's great," he muttered. "Now if you don't mind, I'm going back to sleep."

"No, you're not." Ramata seized her cousin's hand and dragged him out into the middle of the yard. "What do you see, Yusuf, when you lift your eyes from the sand?"

Yusuf glanced up. "The sky," he said.

"Exactly!" Ramata danced excitedly from foot to foot. "Now face the dawn."

She grabbed Yusuf's head and twisted it eastward. Above the horizon, pink and purple colors announced the rising sun. Above that, a well-known constellation of stars was still visible in the dawn sky. It was Ali the Warrior, his starry sword glimmering

"Lift your eyes from the dust-dry sand to summer's breaking dawn," chanted Ramata. "Think, Yusuf! What rises in the east in summer, just before the sun?'

Yusuf scratched his head. "The warrior?" he asked.

"Exactly!" Ramata cried. "And here's the second bit: *'Dry lips may drink from the crooked hand beneath the giant's sword.'"*

Yusuf smiled slowly. "He has a sword in his belt," he said, pointing at the warrior. "But what's the crooked hand?"

"I don't know," said Ramata, her eyes shining. "But I'm going to follow Ali's sword and find out. And you're coming with me."

Yusuf sighed and put his sandals on.

CHAPTER 4

Grandma was thrilled when she heard about the children's quest. She said she would travel with them, and Ramata had no choice but to agree. Ramata suspected that Grandma wanted to keep a close eye on them, but even Ramata had to admit that Grandma's knowledge of the old ways might be a help. They decided to set out at dawn the next morning.

When dawn rolled around, even the donkey seemed excited by the preparations for the journey. Maybe he sensed the hopeful spring in Ramata's step as she put on his harness and padded it carefully with folded rice sacks, before she loaded up an empty barrel and a hose.

Before they set off, Yusuf tied a metal rod onto a length of string. He held the string up high to line it up with Ali's sword. Then he looked to see where it met the horizon.

"There," he said, pointing. "We need to head for the second dune left of the baobab tree."

There was only one container of water left in the village, but the elders insisted that the children take it with them.

Ramata's mother handed Ramata the family's flashlight. "In case you end up traveling at night," she explained.

The villagers wished them luck and waved, and the three explorers set off toward the shimmering sands of the Gourma desert. Ramata and Grandma sat on the cart, and Yusuf walked alongside. Before long, they were deep in the desert, and the village of Simbi was a distant speck on the western horizon.

At midday they reached the dune that Yusuf had pointed out. They led the donkey up to the ridge and looked around them for signs of water: animals, grass, or buzzing flies. But all they saw was sand.

Grandma opened the container of water and passed it to Yusuf. "Drink well," she said. "If we limit ourselves to tiny sips, we'll soon get tired, and then we'll go crazy and die."

Yusuf took a few big swigs and passed the container to Ramata. When the water was finished, Yusuf climbed up onto the cart, and Ramata took her turn walking.

They trudged along the ridge of the dune, down the windward slope and up another one. The stars had long disappeared, so instead they used the sun to navigate, keeping their shadows over their left shoulders.

"So what do you think the 'crooked hand' is?" asked Yusuf.

"It must be something you can drink from," said Grandma. "An oasis, maybe, or a river."

"How will we know when we're close?" asked Yusuf.

"Look out for birds flying in circles," Grandma said. "An oasis always attracts birds."

As the afternoon wore on, a mountain loomed into view.

"That," said Ramata, pointing, "is our last chance of finding water. From the top of the mountain, we'll be able to see for miles around. If there's an oasis anywhere nearby, we'll definitely spot it. And if there's not . . ."

She trailed off into silence. The whole village was relying on them. Failure was not an option, and she knew it.

CHAPTER 5

Two hours later, thirsty and exhausted, the travelers arrived at the foot of the mountain.

"You stay here, Grandma," said Ramata. "Make sure Donkey doesn't wander off. We'll climb the mountain and try to locate the crooked hand."

The children made their way around to the east side of the mountain. It was much cooler in the shade, out of the sun's heat. They kicked their shoes off and began to climb.

The east face was split down the middle by a deep crevice. Ramata squeezed into the crack and edged her way up. There were good handholds and footholds all the way up, so it was not hard to climb. Yusuf followed close behind, panting and muttering as he went. At last, they reached the mountain peak. They rested briefly, then stood up and looked around.

"Oh, no," breathed Yusuf. "This isn't good."

They could see for many miles in every direction, but there was no sign of water at all. Nothing but dry dunes and dead trees as far as the eye could see.

Ramata stayed
silent. She knew that
if she tried to speak, she
would cry, and she did not want to do that.
She slumped back on the rock and stared
dry-eyed at the cloudless, rainless sky.

This desert journey, which had begun in
such excitement, had come to nothing. And
now, with their water container empty, how
would they ever get back home to Simbi?

As she lay there, a red-chested sunbird
flew overhead, once, twice, and then a third
time. It seemed to be circling.

Ramata quickly sat upright. The bird gave
her hope. "Look up, Yusuf," she gasped.

The sunbird circled a few more times,
and then it landed on the mountaintop and
looked at the children with interest.

Down at the bottom of the mountain,
Grandma was yelling what sounded
like "fingers!"

"What are you screeching about,
Grandma?" shouted Yusuf.

"I just walked around the mountain!"
Grandma shrieked back. "That crack you
climbed up—there are three others like it!
You see what this mountain looks like? Five
fingers, pointing up to the sky."

"I don't believe it," whispered Ramata.
"Do you think . . . the mountain could be
the crooked hand?"

The sunbird flew away from them and disappeared down a wide hole. Down it went, through layer upon layer of rock, and the children rushed after it, grazing their knees and elbows but hardly caring. Ramata seized the family flashlight from her pocket and flicked it on, heart pounding in her chest. Desperate not to lose the bird, they moved quickly, skittering down through the mountain like rock lizards.

Far down, the shaft widened, and the children tumbled out into what seemed to be a natural cave inside the mountain. To their left was a glorious circle of sunlight shining through an entrance to the cave. To their right stood the red-chested sunbird.

The bird hopped up onto a narrow ledge and lowered its neck to drink.

There before them was a natural spring: clear, cool water emerging from the rock and cascading down into the belly of the mountain, as it had done for hundreds of years. They gazed, transfixed, while the sunbird drank, and then with cries of joy they flung themselves forward and gulped great mouthfuls of water from the flow.

CHAPTER 6

It was late at night when the weary
three arrived back home in Simbi. As soon
as the thirsty villagers heard the rattle of
donkey cart wheels, they jumped to their
feet and ran to greet the travelers.

"How did it go?" the villagers asked. "Did
you find the crooked hand?"

Grinning all over their faces, Ramata and
Yusuf told their story. The villagers listened
enthralled, gasping at the difficulty of the
journey and finally cheering in delight.

"Once we found the spring, the rest was easy," Ramata concluded. "Yusuf fetched the hose and we used it to channel the water down the side of the mountain. Grandma made sure that Donkey was standing in the right spot, and the water flowed straight into our barrel!"

The villagers drank their fill from the barrel, and then they started to dance and sing. The children felt themselves swept off the ground and hoisted onto their aunts' and uncles' shoulders. Somebody was even carrying Grandma, whirling her 'round and 'round delightedly. The village was saved, and it was time to celebrate.

"We'll go back tomorrow and fill another barrel," Yusuf called to Ramata. "There's enough water there for everyone in Simbi!"

"Enough for Houndi too," said Ramata. "They let us use their pump when water was short, so now we'll let them use our spring—the spring of the crooked hand!"

"The spring of the crooked hand," sang the villagers. *"The spring of the crooked hand! Lift your eyes from the dust-dry sand to the spring of the crooked hand!"*